DISCOVER
YOUR
INNER
CONFIDENCE

"Believe you can and you're halfway there."

Kathryn & Ross Petras

WORKMAN PUBLISHING · NEW YORK

Workman
Workman Publishing
Hachette Book Group, Inc.
1290 Avenue of the Americas
New York, NY 10104
workman.com

Workman is an imprint of Workman Publishing, a division of Hachette Book Group, Inc. The Workman name and logo are registered trademarks of Hachette Book Group, Inc.

Design by Reagan Ruff

The publisher is not responsible for websites (or their content) that are not owned by the publisher.

Workman books may be purchased in bulk for business, educational, or promotional use. For information, please contact your local bookseller or the Hachette Book Group Special Markets Department at special.markets@hbgusa.com.

Library of Congress Cataloging-in-Publication Data
Names: Petras, Kathryn author | Petras, Ross author
Title: Believe you can and you're halfway there / Kathryn & Ross Petras.
Description: First edition. | New York : Workman Publishing, 2025. | Summary: A collection of musings to motivate and inspire readers in need of a dose of self-confidence or a quick pick-me-up—Provided by publisher.
Identifiers: LCCN 2024022119 (print) | LCCN 2024022120 (ebook) | ISBN 9781523525966 (paperback) | ISBN 9781523525980 (epub)
Subjects: LCSH: Self-confidence—Quotations, maxims, etc. | Self-actualization (Psychology—Quotations, maxims, etc.
Classification: LCC BF575.S39 P485 2025 (print) | LCC BF575.S39 (ebook) | DDC 158.1—dc23/eng/20241023
LC record available at https://lccn.loc.gov/2024022119
LC ebook record available at https://lccn.loc.gov/2024022120

First Edition May 2025

Printed in China on responsibly sourced paper.

10 9 8 7 6 5 4 3 2 1

INTRODUCTION

We all want to be the type of person who marches into a meeting brimming with self-confidence, who meets new people without thinking, "What do they think about me?", who calmly looks over a room when making a killer speech and isn't intimidated by all those eyes staring back, who doesn't fret about what to say on that tricky interview or first date.

But all too often, crippling self-doubt creeps in. We tell ourselves, "I can't do it!"

This book answers back, "Yes, you can!"

And better yet, it shows you how.

"Believe you can, and you're halfway there." is a collection of thoughts and musings, motivation, and inspiration from a wide range of people—philosophers to film directors, novelists to rappers, business executives to astronauts. As diverse as they are, they share a common bond: Like all of us, they've dealt with

self-doubts. They've questioned themselves, wondered if they've got what it takes, faced adversity . . . and they triumphed. In these pages, they share their secrets. Their words allow us to look inside of ourselves and find that inner strength, that, "I can do it!" fire that dwells within all of us. It's the perfect pick-me-up for those days when you're feeling less than assured, and it's a shot in the arm when you need a little extra dose of self-confidence.

As Dolly Parton once said, "The magic is inside you, there ain't no crystal ball."

We hope this book reminds you of your magic.

—*Kathryn & Ross Petras*
New York City

I know how it looks. But just start. Nothing is insurmountable.

—**Lin-Manuel Miranda**, *playwright*

The scariest moment is always just before you start.

—Stephen King, *writer*

[He said] don't let them take you over. Walk into the room knowing you are the best. Shoulders back, chin up. Their attitudes will totally change.

—**Misty Copeland**, *dancer*

I am lucky that whatever fear I have inside me, my desire to win is always stronger.

—**Serena Williams,** *athlete*

Believe in yourself
and there will come
a day when others will
have no choice but to
believe with you.

—**Cynthia Kersey**, *writer*

If you have no confidence in self you are twice defeated in the race of life. With confidence, you have won even before you have started.

—Marcus Mosiah Garvey Jr., *activist*

It's easy to quit, right? But tomorrow, how do you feel?

—**Ed Viesturs,** *mountain climber*

Be magnificent.
Life's short.
Get out there.
You can do it.
Everyone can
do it. Everyone.

—Andy Serkis, *actor*

Anyone who ever gave you confidence, you owe them a lot.

—**Truman Capote**, *writer*

For one year, I would say yes to all the things that scared me. Anything that made me nervous, took me out of my comfort zone, I forced myself to say yes to. Did I want to speak in public? No, but yes. Did I want to be on live TV? No, but yes. Did I want to try acting? No, no, no, but yes, yes, yes. And a crazy thing happened: the very act of doing the thing that scared me undid the fear.

—Shonda Rhimes, *producer/screenwriter*

If there is
nothing to ask
permission for,
then don't ask
for permission.

—**Ava DuVernay**, *film director*

You should never be surprised when someone treats you with respect. You should expect it.

—**Sarah Dessen**, *writer*

The reason birds can fly and we can't is simply that they have perfect faith, for to have faith is to have wings.

—**J. M. Barrie**, *writer*

Just stop thinking, worrying, looking over your shoulder, wondering, doubting, fearing, hurting, hoping for some easy way out, struggling, grasping, confusing, itching, scratching, mumbling, bumbling, grumbling, humbling, stumbling, numbling, rambling, gambling, tumbling, scumbling, scrambling, hitching, hatching, bitching, moaning, groaning, honing, boning, horse-shitting, hair-splitting, nit-picking, piss-trickling, nose sticking, ass-gouging, eyeball-poking, finger-pointing, alleyway-sneaking, long waiting, small stepping, evil-eyeing, back-scratching, searching, perching, besmirching, grinding, grinding, grinding away at yourself. Stop it and just DO.

—Sol LeWitt, *artist*

Most people with low self-esteem have earned it.

—George Carlin, *comedian*

Confidence can't exist in the absence of insecurity. Every human being is insecure. Every human being is afraid. A person who is willing to actually admit that is actually more confident than the person who refuses to admit it, because it takes courage to admit that you're insecure.

—**Barry Michels,** *psychotherapist*

I own my story.... I own my failures.... I'm not interested in being perfect.

—**Viola Davis**, *actor*

You don't actually need confidence or good self-esteem to be successful. You just need to have courage . . . You can accomplish so many things with a negative outlook and low self-esteem if you just do it over and over and over again. You have to have balls and resilience.

—Lela Loren, *actor*

I have learned over the years that when one's mind is made up, this diminishes fear; knowing what must be done does away with fear.

—Rosa Parks, *activist*

It's not your job
to be likable.
It's your job
to be yourself.
Someone will
like you anyway.

—**Chimamanda Ngozi Adichie,** *writer*

As a coach said once, "You can't fake confidence." You only get it through experience. I think a lot of youthful passion is actually lack of confidence. You're having to double your energy because you really don't have, you know, experience. And experience can kind of lighten you up a little bit, so that you're thinking, "OK, maybe the sky isn't falling. We can fix this problem. We will fix it."

—**Richard Linklater**, *film director*

Whatever we believe about ourselves and our ability comes true for us.

—Susan L. Taylor, *editor/journalist*

You are your best thing.

—**Toni Morrison**, *writer*

When I ask if you're talented, you'd better say yes. Not in a boasting sort of way, just a quiet confidence: "Yes, I'm talented. I know I am." You need that.

—**Bryan Cranston,** *actor*

Love yourself first, and everything else falls in line. You really have to love yourself to get anything done in this world.

—**Lucille Ball**, *comedian/producer*

One important
key to success is
self-confidence.
An important key
to self-confidence
is preparation.

—Arthur Ashe, *athlete*

'Tisn't life that matters! 'Tis the courage you bring to it.

—**Hugh Walpole**, *writer*

Impossible is just a big word thrown around by small men who find it easier to live in the world they've been given than to explore the power they have to change it. Impossible is not a fact. It's an opinion. Impossible is not a declaration. It's a dare. Impossible is potential. Impossible is temporary. Impossible is nothing.

—**Aimee Lehto**, *copywriter,*
in collaboration with
Boyd Coyner, *creative director*

Confidence is
10 percent hard
work and 90 percent
delusion—just
thinking foolishly that
you will be able to do
what you want to do.

—**Tina Fey**, *actor*

Nothing is better for self-esteem than survival.

—Martha Gellhorn, *journalist*

[I want] people to walk around delusional about how great they can be, and then to fight so hard for it every day that the lie becomes the truth.

—Lady Gaga, *singer/actor*

If you don't have confidence, you'll always find a way not to win.

—Carl Lewis, *athlete*

If you want to be respected by others, the great thing is to respect yourself. Only by that, only by self-respect, will you compel others to respect you.

—Fyodor Dostoevsky, *writer*

Self-respect cannot be hunted. It cannot be purchased. It is never for sale. It cannot be fabricated out of public relations. It comes to us when we are alone, in quiet moments, in quiet places, when we suddenly realize that, knowing the good, we have done it; knowing the beautiful, we have served it; knowing the truth, we have spoken it.

—Alfred Whitney Griswold, *historian*

The magic is inside you, there ain't no crystal ball.

—Dolly Parton, *musician*

Self-respect permeates every aspect of your lives. If you don't have it for yourselves, you're not gonna get it from anywhere.

—Michael Schiffer, *screenwriter*

Whatever it is that you think you want to do, and whatever it is that you think stands between you and that, stop making excuses. You can do anything.

—Katia Beauchamp, *entrepreneur*

I've finally stopped running away from myself. Who else is there better to be?

—**Goldie Hawn**, *actor*

People respond well to those that are sure of what they want.

—Anna Wintour, *editor*

Self-confidence is the first requisite to great undertakings.

—Samuel Johnson, *writer*

I got to where I am today through determination and hard work, and importantly, by ignoring the people who told me that I couldn't do it, that I wasn't any good, and who claimed that I asked stupid questions.

—**Chiara Mingarelli**, *astrophysicist*

Just because I made it here doesn't mean it was easy. And just because I don't seem overwhelmed doesn't mean I'm not.

—**Jen Wilde,** *writer*

The best way to get approval is not to need it. This is equally true in art and business. And love. And sex. And just about everything else worth having.

—**Hugh MacLeod**, *cartoonist*

You are enough.
You were born
enough. The world
is waiting on you.

—**Elaine Welteroth**, *writer*

I always have a comfortable feeling that nothing is impossible if one applies a certain amount of energy in the right direction. When I want things done, which is always at the last moment, and I am met with such an answer: "It's too late. I hardly think it can be done;" I simply say: "Nonsense! If you want to do it, you can do it. The question is, do you want to do it?"

—Nellie Bly, *journalist*

You're walking along a tightrope, and you must try to keep your balance. When you're feeling particularly secure, you can perform a triple somersault, and when you sense a risk, you draw on your experience so as not to lose your footing. You use emotion sparingly. The more you have worked on the piece, the more you will have got to grips with the technical difficulties and the expressive potential, and the more free you are to leave room for emotion because you know you will always fall on your feet.

—Andrea Bocelli, *singer*

The doing is the thing. The talking and worrying and thinking is not the thing.

—Amy Poehler, *comedian*

Humor comes from self-confidence.

—Rita Mae Brown, *writer*

The measure of achievement is not winning awards.
It's doing something that you appreciate, something you believe is worthwhile. I think of my strawberry souffle. I did that at least twenty-eight times before I finally conquered it.

—**Julia Child**, *chef*

Who the hell said that you no longer had it in you?

—Charles Bukowski, *writer*

For me it's just about that self-confidence and finding what you love and just chasing after it with reckless abandon and never letting anyone tell you that you can't do something. If you have a goal and you set your mind to it, you can absolutely achieve it.

—**Kelley O'Hara**, *athlete*

I am somebody…
I am me. I like
being me, and
I need nobody
to make me
somebody.

—Louis L'Amour, *writer*

If you could only sense
how important you are
to the lives of those you
meet; how important
you can be to people you
may never even dream
of. There is something
of yourself that you
leave at every meeting
with another person.

—**Fred Rogers**, *children's show host*

The root of true confidence grows from unconditional friendship with ourselves, to train in gentleness, and to trust in our natural intelligence to navigate life. Confidence.

—**Pema Chödrön**, *spiritual teacher*

I never thought of losing, but now that it's happened, the only thing is to do it right.

—Muhammad Ali, *athlete*

I feel like I struggled for years to adhere to whoever was in front of the room, that someone's opinion mattered more than my own. We have to strike a balance between the advice we're given, the guidance we're given, and trusting our own individual instincts as artists.

—**David Hallberg,** *artistic director*

Greatness is hearing your truth and speaking it no matter how your voice shakes.

—**Mel Robbins,** *writer*

Doubt kills more dreams than failure ever will.

—Suzy Kassem, *screenwriter*

I cannot agree with those who rank modesty among the virtues. To the logician all things should be seen exactly as they are, and to underestimate one's self is as much a departure from truth as to exaggerate one's own powers.

—Arthur Conan Doyle, *writer*

So you may not always have a comfortable life. And you will not always be able to solve all the world's problems all at once. But don't ever underestimate the impact you can have, because history has shown us that courage can be contagious, and hope can take on a life of its own.

—Michelle Obama, *attorney/writer*

Fear, to a great extent, is born of a story we tell ourselves, and so I chose to tell myself a different story from the one women are told. I decided I was safe. I was strong. I was brave. Nothing could vanquish me.

—Cheryl Strayed, *writer*

To ride a bicycle properly is very like a love affair—chiefly it is a matter of faith. Believe you do it, and the thing is done; doubt, and for the life of you, you cannot.

—H. G. Wells, *writer*

You can't build joy on a feeling of self-loathing.

—**Ram Dass**, *spiritual teacher*

Confidence is that feeling by which the mind embarks in great and honorable courses with a sure hope and trust in itself.

—**Marcus Tullius Cicero**, *statesman*

You alone are enough. You have nothing to prove to anybody.

—**Maya Angelou,** *writer*

Life is not easy for any of us. But what of that? We must have perseverance and, above all, confidence in ourselves. We must believe that we are gifted for something, and that this thing, at whatever cost, must be attained.

—**Marie Curie**, *physicist/chemist*

It is best to act
with confidence,
no matter how
little right you
have to it.

—Lillian Hellman, *playwright/writer*

To be beautiful means to be yourself. You don't need to be accepted by others. You need to accept yourself. When you are born a lotus flower, be a beautiful lotus flower, don't try to be a magnolia flower. If you crave acceptance and recognition and try to change yourself to fit what other people want you to be, you will suffer all your life. True happiness and true power lie in understanding yourself, accepting yourself, having confidence in yourself.

—Thích Nhất Hạnh, *monk/activist*

A man cannot be comfortable without his own approval.

—**Mark Twain**, *writer*

I taught myself confidence.... When I'd walk into a room and feel scared to death, I'd tell myself, "I'm not afraid of anybody." And people believed me. You've got to teach yourself to take over the world.

—Priyanka Chopra, *actor/producer*

When I wake up in the morning, I feel just like any other insecure 24-year-old girl. Then I say, "Bitch, you're Lady Gaga, you get up and walk the walk today."

—Lady Gaga, *singer/actor*

If you hear a voice within you saying, "You are not a painter," *then by all means paint* ... and that voice will be silenced.

—**Vincent van Gogh,** *artist*

If you are taking a risk, what you are really saying is, "I believe in tomorrow and I will be part of it."

—**Linda Ellerbee,** *journalist*

The real winners in life are the people who look at every situation with an expectation that they can make it work or make it better.

—Barbara Pletcher, *business executive*

Put blinders on to those things that conspire to hold you back, especially the ones in your own head.

—Meryl Streep, *actor*

Confidence is just entitlement ... entitlement is simply the belief that you deserve something. Which is great. The hard part is, you'd better make sure you deserve it.

—**Mindy Kaling,** *actor*

You don't become what you want, you become what you believe.

—**Oprah Winfrey,** *media executive*

If I have lost confidence in myself, I have the universe against me.

—Ralph Waldo Emerson, *writer*

It's good to be confident and to know who you are, but it's okay to also not know who you are. It's a fun journey.

—Millie Bobby Brown, *actor*

What's the difference between a smart risk and a foolish one? A smart risk involves assessing the terrain, researching what's up ahead, and pushing beyond your fears. In other words, don't walk out the door thinking you can wing it; that's arrogance. Walk out the door knowing you've put in the work; that's confidence.

—**Gayle King,** *broadcast journalist*

I have gone ahead despite the pounding in the heart that says: Turn back.

—Erica Jong, *writer*

That's the funny thing about confidence … The incorrect amount of it, and nothing will ever happen.

—Robert Downey Jr., *actor*

No one is ever safe. So why not live as much as you can?

—Rita Mae Brown, *writer*

There are moments on the brink,
when you can give yourself
to a lover, or not; give in to
self-doubt, uncertainty, and
admonishment, or not; dive into
a different culture, or not; set sail
for the unknown, or not; walk
out onto a stage, or not . . . Resist
then, and . . . there is only what
might have been.

—Diane Ackerman, *poet/essayist*

I think the best accessory you can wear is confidence.

—Adam Glassman, *creative director/stylist*

Mistakes will be made. Failure will occur. You pick yourself up and carry on.

—**Elizabeth Gilbert**, *writer*

Trust yourself—
you know more
than you think
you do.

—Benjamin Spock, *physician*

Confidence doesn't come out of nowhere. It's a result of something ... hours and days and weeks and years of constant work and dedication.

—Roger Staubach, *athlete*

Let go of the idea that things could have happened differently, as if this life is a Choose Your Own Adventure book and you simply turned to the wrong page. You did the best you could with what you knew—and felt—at the time. Now do better, knowing more.

—Maggie Smith, *poet/writer/editor*

There is only one thing that makes a dream impossible to achieve: the fear of failure.

—**Paulo Coelho**, *writer*

My life changed when I focused on what I was good at, what I liked most about myself, and what made me stand out. Once I learned to like me more than others did, then I didn't have to worry about being the funniest or the most popular or the prettiest. I was the best me and I only ever tried to be that.

—**Issa Rae**, *actor/writer/producer*

Never be bullied into silence. Never allow yourself to be made a victim. Accept no one's definition of your life; define yourself.

—Harvey Fierstein, *actor*

I know not all
that may be
coming, but
be it what it
will, I'll go to
it laughing.

—**Herman Melville**, *writer*

When we can see ourselves as we truly are and accept ourselves, we build the necessary foundation for self-love.

—**bell hooks,** *writer/social critic*

It's not to anybody's best interest to think about how they will be perceived tomorrow. It hurts you in the long run.

—**Bob Dylan**, *musician*

It's a terrible thing, I think, in life to wait until you're ready. I have this feeling now that actually no one is ever ready to do anything. There's almost no such thing as ready. There's only now. And you may as well do it now. I mean, I say that confidently as if I'm about to go bungee jumping or something— I'm not. I'm not a crazed risk taker. But I do think that, generally speaking, now is as good a time as any.

—Hugh Laurie, *actor/comedian*

Confidence is contagious. So is lack of confidence.

—**Vince Lombardi,** *coach*

Go ahead
and believe
that no
one shines
brighter
than you.

—**Demi Lovato,** *singer*

The next time you hesitate before going after something you want, the next time you blush and brush off a compliment, the next time you doubt your place in the world, in the workplace, in your home or in your own skin, say these words to yourself: "I'm worth it." And I know you will always say it like you mean it.

—Viola Davis, *actor*

I think you also get more confident as you get older. You realize what your strengths and your weaknesses are and you're more okay with your weaknesses and you value your strengths more.

—Elisabeth Moss, *actor/producer*

The big lesson in life, baby, is never be scared of anyone or anything.

—**Frank Sinatra**, *singer*

I always did something I was a little not ready to do. I think that's how you grow. When there's that moment of "wow, I'm not really sure I can do this," and you push through those moments, that's when you have a breakthrough.

—**Marissa Mayer**, *entrepreneur*

Nobody will believe in you but yourself so you have to be on your own side.

—**Eline Powell**, *actor*

Get there early and get a seat at the table. If you have an opinion, speak out. Have a voice in your organization and never say I'm sorry. Women are always like, "Oh, I'm sorry." No, you're not sorry. Just say how you feel.

—**Trish Bertuzzi**, *consultant*

The way you tell your story to yourself matters.

—**Amy Cuddy,** *social psychologist*

We all think everybody else has got a big club, while we've got a tiny Q-Tip behind us . . . and we all think we've missed out on the secrets of life, and everybody else has got it. . . . But the wonderful secret is that we're all equally afraid and uncertain, and that, that isn't a bad thing; it's a wonderful thing.

—Stephen Fry, *actor/writer*

You are there for a reason. You are there because you deserve to be in that room at that time . . . You need to somehow force it into your brain: "I'm badass. I deserve to be here."

—**Gigi Hadid**, *model*

For every story that you have about why you can't do something, there's another story you can tell yourself about why you can.

—**Kindra Hall**, *writer*

Once you make the decision to be comfortable with yourself and you don't really care what anybody else thinks, you exude a confidence that people gravitate towards.

—Michael B. Jordan, *actor*

"Lucky" implies that I was handed something I did not earn, that I did not work hard for. . . . I am not lucky. You know what I am? I am smart, I am talented, I take advantage of the opportunities that come my way and I work really, really hard. Don't call me lucky. Call me a badass.

—**Shonda Rhimes**, *producer/screenwriter*

Stay afraid, but do it anyway. What's important is the action. You don't have to wait to be confident. Just do it and eventually the confidence will follow.

—**Carrie Fisher**, *actress/writer*

The unknown is what it is. And to be frightened of it is what sends everybody scurrying around chasing dreams, illusions, wars, peace, love, hate, all that— it's all illusion. Unknown is what it is. Accept that it's unknown and it's plain sailing. Everything is unknown—then you're ahead of the game. That's what it is. Right?

—**John Lennon**, *musician*

Great people do things before they're ready. They do things before they know they can do it. . . . Doing what you're afraid of, getting out of your comfort zone, taking risks like that— that's what life is. You might be really good. You might find out something about yourself that's really special and if you're not good, who cares? You tried something. Now you know something about yourself.

—Amy Poehler, *comedian*

"Do you mean," Lidi said in a tone of deep existential disgust, "that we have to *believe* in it to make it work?"

"You have to believe in yourself in order to act, don't you?" Tai said.

"No," the navigator said. "Absolutely not. I don't believe in myself. I *know* some things. Enough to go on."

—Ursula K. Le Guin, *writer*

I guess I was never much in awe of anybody. I think you have to have that attitude if you're going to go far.

—**Bob Gibson**, *athlete*

If you believe in what you're saying, if you believe in what you're doing, you'll be more effective, more passionate, and more authentic in everything you do.

—**Seth Goldman**, *entrepreneur*

Before you diagnose yourself with depression or low self-esteem, first make sure that you are not, in fact, just surrounded by assholes.

—William Gibson, *writer*

A man's own self is the last person to believe in him, and is harder to cheat than the rest of the world.

—George Bernard Shaw, *writer*

Some people say
I have attitude—
maybe I do…but
I think you have to.
You have to believe
in yourself when
no one else does—
that makes you a
winner right there.

—Venus Williams, *athlete*

I do not trouble my spirit to vindicate itself or be understood.

—**Walt Whitman**, *writer*

Be your own artist, and always be confident in what you're doing. If you're not going to be confident, you might as well not be doing it.

—Aretha Franklin, *singer*

To convince others, you have to convince yourself.

—**Louise Bourgeois,** *artist*

Be gentle and kind with yourself. Confidence is something that takes courage in a world that doesn't always support who we are.

—Tracee Ellis Ross, *actor*

Think of something you have always wanted to do but have avoided because you fear it could be embarrassing. Now clear your mind and give it a go.

—**Alex Malley,** *business executive*

The term "confidence trick" has a bad meaning, but it shouldn't. In culture, confidence is the currency of value. Once you surrender the idea of intrinsic, objective value, you start asking the question "if the value isn't in there, where does it come from?" It's obviously from the transaction: it's the product of the quality of a relationship between me, the observer, and something else. So how is that relationship stimulated, enriched, given value? By creating an atmosphere of confidence where I am ready to engage with and perhaps surrender to the world it suggests.

—**Brian Eno,** *musician/composer*

One of the things I learned the hard way was that it doesn't pay to get discouraged. Keeping busy and making optimism a way of life can restore your faith in yourself.

—**Lucille Ball**, *comedian/producer*

Optimism is the faith that leads to achievement. Nothing can be done without hope and confidence.

—**Helen Keller**, *writer/activist*

Once you realize there is life after mistakes, you gain a self-confidence that never goes away.

—**Bob Schieffer**, *journalist*

I do the very best I know how—the very best I can; and I mean to keep doing so until the end. If the end brings me out all right, what is said against me won't amount to anything. If the end brings me out wrong, ten angels swearing I was right would make no difference.

—Abraham Lincoln, *president*

You have within you right now, everything you need to deal with whatever the world can throw at you.

—**Brian Tracy,** *motivational speaker/writer*

I don't like to gamble, but if there's one thing I'm willing to bet on, it's myself.

—**Beyoncé**, *singer/songwriter*

Inaction breeds doubt and fear. Action breeds confidence and courage. If you want to conquer fear, do not sit home and think about it. Go out and get busy.

—Dale Carnegie,
writer/motivational coach

Confidence makes us beautiful, and it comes from accepting yourself. The moment you accept yourself, it makes everything better.

—Diane von Furstenberg, *designer*

Just be yourself, there is no one better.

—Taylor Swift, *singer/songwriter*

You are the sky. Everything else—it's just the weather.

—**Pema Chödrön**, *spiritual teacher*

Belief is very important. It's like when you are riding a horse and you want it to go to the left, you look to the left first and then pull the horse's head. As a human being it is the same thing: wherever you put your attention is probably where you are going to find yourself.

—**Colin Farrell**, *actor*

If I could go back and tell my younger self one thing it would be this:

"Abby, you were never Little Red Riding Hood. You were always the wolf."

—**Abby Wambach,** *athlete*

My daughter made an amazing jump in the pool the other day. I said, "You're so brave." She said, "No, I was scared." I said, "That's why you're brave. If you weren't scared, you wouldn't be brave at all. You'd just be dumb."

—**Mary Louise Parker,** *actor*

If I can't make it through one door, I'll go through another door—or I'll make a door. Something terrific will come no matter how dark the present.

—Rabindranath Tagore, *writer*

Believe it can be done. When you believe something can be done, really believe, your mind will find the ways to do it. Believing a solution paves the way to solution.

—David J. Schwartz,
writer/motivational coach

No matter how good you were, someone was better. Live according to that knowledge, and you would never grow so confident that you became sloppy.

—**Brandon Sanderson**, *writer*

Confidence
is a fine trait.
Overconfidence
isn't.

—**Laurell K. Hamilton**, *writer*

Putting yourself out there is hard, but it's so worth it. I don't think anyone who has ever spoken out, or stood up or had a brave moment, has regretted it. It's empowering and confidence-building and inspiring. Not only to other people, but to yourself.

—**Megan Rapinoe**, *athlete*

My legacy is
that I stayed on
course . . . from
the beginning to
the end, because
I believed in
something
inside of me.

—Tina Turner, *singer*

I learned this, at least,
by my experiment:
that if one advances
confidently in the
direction of his
dreams, and endeavors
to live the life which
he has imagined,
he will meet with a
success unexpected
in common hours.

—Henry David Thoreau,
naturalist/writer

I am the greatest. I said that even before I knew I was. I figured that if I said it enough, I would convince the world that I really was the greatest.

—**Muhammad Ali**, *athlete*

An amazing thing happens when you stop seeking approval and validation: you find it. People are naturally drawn like magnets to those who know who they are and cannot be shaken!

—**Mandy Hale**, *writer*

When you start to rewrite the story of not-mattering, you start to find a new center. You remove yourself from other people's mirrors and begin speaking more fully from your own experience, your own knowing place. You become better able to attach to your pride and more readily step over all the despites. It doesn't remove the obstacles, but I've found that it helps to shrink them. It helps you to count your victories, even the small ones, and know that you're doing okay.

—Michelle Obama, *attorney/writer*

I never realized how much of leadership is learning to sound confident when you're actually terrified.

—Rick Riordan, *writer*

I do believe that inside each of us, inside our imaginative lives, dwells every possibility in the human journey. It is a matter of access, I suppose. And the courage to access. I think we all have the same weapons: patience, imagination, hope, and the ability to be crucified and yet resurrect.

—**Shobha Rao**, *writer*

There's a time in your life where you're not quite sure where you are. You think everything's perfect, but it's not perfect. . . . Then one day you wake up and you can't quite picture yourself in the situation you're in. But the secret is, if you can picture yourself doing anything in life, you can do it.

—**Tom DeLonge**, *musician*

If you do
not believe
you can do
it then you
have no
chance at all.

—**Arsène Wenger,** *soccer manager*

Life for both sexes—
and I looked at them,
shouldering their way along
the pavement—is arduous,
difficult, a perpetual
struggle. It calls for gigantic
courage and strength. More
than anything, perhaps,
creatures of illusion as we
are, it calls for confidence
in oneself. Without self-
confidence we are as babes
in the cradle.

—Virginia Woolf, *writer*

When I stopped trying to BE SOMEBODY or FIX myself, and instead gave myself grace to be who I was, everything changed. I started to recognize and love my uniqueness and my authentic, true self. Once that happened, confidence came rushing in.

—Kim Gravel, *business executive/writer*

It is only necessary
to have courage,
for strength without
self-confidence
is useless.

—**Giacomo Casanova**, *adventurer/writer*

A huge light-bulb moment for me personally has been noticing that I need both periods of self-confidence and self-doubt to produce my best work.

—**Alice Boyes,** *psychologist*

The better you feel about yourself, the less you feel the need to show off.

—**Robert Hand**, *astrologer/historian*

You have no responsibility to live up to what other people think you ought to accomplish. I have no responsibility to be like they expect me to be. It's their mistake, not my failing.

—Richard P. Feynman, *physicist*

You are not
a drop in the
ocean. You are
the entire ocean
in a drop.

—Rumi, *poet*

You better not compromise yourself. It's all you've got.

—**Janis Joplin,** *singer*

Man often becomes what he believes himself to be. . . . If I keep on saying to myself that I cannot do a certain thing, it is possible that I may end by really becoming incapable of doing it. On the contrary, if I have the belief that I can do it, I shall surely acquire the capacity to do it even if I may not have it at the beginning.

—Mohandas K. Gandhi, *humanitarian*

Find out who you are and do it on purpose.

—Dolly Parton, *singer*

The self-confidence of the warrior is not the self-confidence of the average man. The average man seeks certainty in the eyes of the onlooker and calls that self-confidence. The warrior seeks impeccability in his own eyes and calls that humbleness. The average man is hooked to his fellow men, while the warrior is hooked only to himself.

—Carlos Castaneda, *writer*

I have often wondered how it is that every man loves himself more than all the rest of men, but yet sets less value on his own opinion of himself than on the opinion of others.

—**Marcus Aurelius**, *emperor*

I am only one,
But still I am one.
I cannot do everything,
But still I can do something;
And because I cannot do everything,
I will not refuse to do the
something that I can do.

—Edward Everett Hale, *writer/historian*

"Baby," I said. "I'm a genius but nobody knows it but me."

—**Charles Bukowski**, *writer*

Confidence literally starts from yourself. You have to go look in the mirror at yourself. If you don't like what you see, you're going to give off that energy.

—**Megan Thee Stallion**, *rapper*

Just speak very loudly and quickly, and state your position with utter conviction, as the French do, and you'll have a marvelous time!

—**Julia Child**, *chef*

It would be a shame to waste our snippet of time on this planet being afraid.

—**Deborah Landau,** *poet/essayist*

To become more successful, don't change who you are. Become more of who you are.

—**Sally Hogshead,**
writer/advertising executive

There have been so many people who have said to me, "You can't do that," but I've had an innate belief that they were wrong. Be unwavering and relentless in your approach.

—Halle Berry, *actor*

You gain strength, courage, and confidence by every experience in which you really stop to look fear in the face. You are able to say to yourself, "I lived through this horror. I can take the next thing that comes along."

—**Eleanor Roosevelt**, *humanitarian*

Let others determine your worth and you're already lost, because no one wants people worth more than themselves.

—Peter V. Brett, *writer*

I think vulnerability is . . . the cornerstone of confidence. Unless you can allow yourself to take the risk, to be open, to live as a whole-hearted person. Do that and you recognize that you're just like everybody else, and that gives you the confidence to be yourself. Which is all you really need in life: To be more of yourself.

—Oprah Winfrey, *media executive*

Trust thyself:
every heart
vibrates to that
iron string.

—**Ralph Waldo Emerson**, *writer*

All you need is confidence in yourself. There is no living thing that is not afraid when it faces danger. The true courage is in facing danger when you are afraid, and that kind of courage you have in plenty.

—L. Frank Baum, *writer*

I don't like myself, I'm crazy about myself.

—Mae West, *actor*

Our inability to tolerate uncertainty, and our inability to tolerate disapproval and judgment. That holds people back to such a huge degree. We're so afraid of what people think of us. Again, when you love your shadow and feel that you're in an unbreakable alliance with your shadow, then you can go out there and say and do anything you want. If someone disapproves of you, "Fine. I respect that. It's fine, but it doesn't change who I am because my identity rests in the relationship with my shadow, rather than in my relationship with some outside person."

—**Barry Michels,** *psychotherapist*

People who say they don't care what people think are usually desperate to have people think they don't care what people think.

—**George Carlin**, *comedian*

It takes courage to grow up and turn out to be who you really are.

—**E. E. Cummings,** *poet*

When you act confident, you will start feeling confident.

—Vanessa Yakobson, *business executive*

I love having stage-fright because it's a reminder that I'm trying something new, that I'm gonna risk something, and hopefully, in the process, learn something.

—**Lupita Nyong'o**, *actor*

The secret to doing anything is believing that you can do it. Anything that you believe you can do strong enough, you can do. Anything. As long as you believe.

—**Bob Ross**, *artist/TV show host*

Throughout your journey and throughout your life, you're going to be faced with challenges. Rely on your knowledge. Do not doubt yourself.

—Jackie Joyner-Kersee, *athlete*

She lacks confidence, she craves admiration insatiably. She lives on the reflections of herself in the eyes of others. She does not dare to be herself.

—Anaïs Nin,
*writer, on the price we pay
for lack of confidence*

There are people who go to museums who look at paintings and think: Shit, I could've done that. But you didn't.

—Viggo Mortensen, *actor*

Never be limited by other people's limited imaginations.

—Mae Jemison,
engineer/physician/astronaut

You've got to have confidence in the very thing that makes you unique—then wait for the world to catch up.

—Lindsey Stirling, *violinist*

The way to develop self-confidence is to do the thing you fear and get a record of successful experiences behind you.

—**William Jennings Bryan**, *statesman*

Obstacles can't stop you. Problems can't stop you. Most of all, other people can't stop you. Only you can stop you.

—**Jeffrey Gitomer,** *salesperson/writer*

If you are insecure, guess what? The rest of the world is too. Do not overestimate the competition and underestimate yourself. You are better than you think.

—Timothy Ferriss, *entrepreneur*

The most
important
opinion
you have is
the opinion
you have
of yourself.

—Zig Ziglar, *writer/salesperson*

Low self-confidence isn't a life sentence. Self-confidence can be learned, practiced, and mastered—just like any other skill. Once you master it, everything in your life will change for the better.

—Barrie Davenport, *lifestyle coach*

Believe in yourself
and all that you are.
Know that there is
something inside
you greater than
any obstacle.

—**Christian D. Larson,** *teacher*

A person who doubts himself
is like a man who would enlist
in the ranks of his enemies and
bear arms against himself. He
makes his failure certain by
himself being the first person
to be convinced of it.

—Alexandre Dumas, *writer*

My self-confidence comes from the fact that I have discovered my own dimensions. It does not behoove me to make myself smaller than I am.

—**Edith Södergran**, *poet*

With time you grow up! That's all! You just grow up and realize that everybody's opinion doesn't matter! You just start to care less.

—Alicia Keys, *singer/songwriter*

Have the courage to follow your heart and intuition. They somehow already know what you truly want to become. Everything else is secondary.

—**Steve Jobs,** *entrepreneur*

Work hard, know your sh-t, show your sh-t, and then be entitled.

—Mindy Kaling, *actor*

Confidence is going after Moby Dick in a rowboat and taking tartar sauce with you.

—Zig Ziglar, *writer/salesperson*

What's wrong with this egotism? If a man doesn't delight in himself and the force in him and feel that he and it are wonders, how is all life to become important to him?

—**Sherwood Anderson**, *writer*

The biggest epiphany was that the best I could do was actually be me.

—Tracee Ellis Ross, *actor*

Whatever you want
to do, just do it. . . .
Making a damn
fool of yourself is
absolutely essential.

—**Gloria Steinem**, *activist/journalist*

The greatest bit of advice I've ever received was "Don't worry, no one else knows what they're doing either."

—**Ricky Gervais,** *comedian*

Have confidence that if you have done a little thing well, you can do a bigger thing well too.

—**David Storey**, *playwright*

Confidence is preparation. Everything else is beyond your control.

—Richard Kline, *actor*

I began to recognize a source of power within myself that comes from the knowledge that while it is most desirable not to be afraid, learning to put fear into a perspective gave me great strength.

—**Audre Lorde,** *writer/professor*

Optimism is a perfectly legitimate response to failure.

—Stephen King, *writer*

People with high assurance in their capabilities approach difficult tasks as challenges to be mastered rather than as threats to be avoided.

—Albert Bandura, *psychologist*

"Sometimes I think you believe in me more than I do," said the boy.
    "You'll catch up," said the horse.

—**Charlie Mackesy,** *artist/writer*

Who you are today . . . that's who you are.

Be brave.

Be amazing.

Be worthy.

And every single time you get the chance?

Stand up in front of people.

Let them see you. Speak. Be heard.

Go ahead and have the dry mouth.

Let your heart beat so, so fast.

Watch everything move in slow motion.

So what. You what?

You pass out, you die, you poop?

No.

(And this is really the only lesson you'll ever need to know.) You take it in.

—Shonda Rhimes, *producer/screenwriter*

Never let the fear of striking out keep you from swinging.

—Babe Ruth, *athlete*

Confidence is not "they will like me." Confidence instead is "I'll be fine if they don't."

—**Christine Grimmie**, *singer*

Overpower.
Overtake.
Overcome.

—Serena Williams, *athlete*

You are a very special person. There is only one like you in the whole world. There's never been anyone exactly like you before, and there never will be again.

—**Fred Rogers,** *children's show host*

Become amazing, and be happy.

—Demi Lovato, *singer*

Do you know what luck is? Luck is thinking you're lucky. If you think you're lucky, you are.

—**John Mellencamp**, *musician*

I think in your life there's a moment when the door opens and you need to walk through the door then. You can't say then, "Well, I'll go through it two years from now. I'll do it, I'll save up some money . . ." Because by then the door will be closed.

—**David Sedaris,** *comedian/writer*

I have self-doubt. I have insecurity. I have fear of failure. I have nights when I show up at the arena and I'm like, "My back hurts, my feet hurt, my knees hurt. I don't have it. I just want to chill." We all have self-doubt. You don't deny it, but you also don't capitulate to it. You embrace it.

—**Kobe Bryant**, *athlete*

Stop worrying about how it's gonna happen and start believing that it will.

—Michaela Olexova, *creative entrepreneur*

Never let a soul bring you down, all it takes is a little self-love and confidence to bring your strength right back to the surface. Where it belongs.

—**Lady Gaga**, *singer/actor*

Don't wait until everything is just right. It will never be perfect. There will always be challenges, obstacles, and less than perfect conditions. So what. Get started now. With each step you take, you will grow stronger and stronger, more and more skilled, more and more self-confident, and more and more successful.

—Mark Victor Hansen,
writer/motivational speaker

Skill and confidence are an unconquered army.

—George Herbert, *poet/orator*

My theory is that if you look confident you can pull off anything—even if you have no clue what you're doing.

—Jessica Alba, *actor/entrepreneur*

If people don't like the pictures, I don't care. To me, there's only one point of view: that's mine.

—**Harry Benson,** *photographer*

As is our confidence, so is our capacity.

—**William Hazlitt**, *essayist*

The more I heard that I couldn't make it, the more I was determined to do it.

—Archie Griffin, *athlete*

Always remember, Goliath was a 40-point favorite over David.

—James "Shug" Jordan, *athlete/coach*

It's the time to buckle down and work positively as much as you can. Just think, "All right, there's nothing I can do about that right now. But I can do my best in my little circle. So if I do that, maybe you'll do your best and we'll get through this."

—**Betty White**, *actor*

Action is the cure for low confidence.

—Barrie Davenport, *lifestyle coach*

It can't last forever. Others have thought such things in bad times before this, and they were always right, they did get out one way or another, and it didn't last forever.

—**Margaret Atwood**, *writer*

Believe you can, and you're halfway there.

—Theodore Roosevelt, *president*

If being an egomaniac means I believe in what I do and in my art or music, then in that respect you can call me that . . . I believe in what I do, and I'll say it.

—John Lennon, *musician*

I've been absolutely terrified every moment of my life and I've never let it keep me from a single thing that I wanted to do.

—**Georgia O'Keeffe**, *artist*

The worst enemy to creativity is self-doubt.

—Sylvia Plath, *writer*

It's just so boring, it's so boring listening to false modesty. I've worked for many, many years so I'm really enjoying that my hard work has paid off. . . . I think you should know your worth!

—**Denise Gough**, *actor*

You can receive all the compliments in the world, but that won't do a thing unless you believe it yourself.

—**Criss Jami**, *writer*

No matter how much
you strive for perfection,
you will fall at some
point. Accepting that as
part of your journey and
not letting it rattle your
confidence are critical
elements to growth.
There are no failures, only
lessons to be learned.

—**Shannon Petteruti,** *business executive*

The only limit to our realization of tomorrow will be our doubts of today.

—Franklin D. Roosevelt, *president*

When you have confidence, you can have a lot of fun. And when you have fun, you can do amazing things.

—Joe Namath, *athlete*

The day I was born is the day I became worthy. And I say that to everybody out there—there is absolutely *nothing* you have to do it for. If anyone is telling you otherwise, they're telling you a straight-up lie.

—Viola Davis, *actor*

Badassery, I'm discovering, is a new level of confidence—in both yourself and those around you. I now feel like I can see so many amazing things about myself and the people around me. It's as if before, by hiding and worrying and being unhappy, I was not looking at the people around me and seeing how truly gifted and amazing they are. There was certainly nothing in me that could have been positive and uplifting or inspiring to them. Not when I was so busy hiding and trying to be smaller and a nothing.

I've started to think we are like mirrors. What you are gets reflected back to you. What you see in yourself, you may see in others, and what others see in you, they may see in themselves.

—Shonda Rhimes, *producer/screenwriter*

Don't be afraid of fear. . . . Throw caution to the winds, look fear straightaway in its ugly face, and barge forward. And when you get past it, turn around and give it a good swift kick in the ass.

—Helen Mirren, *actor*

It doesn't matter if we were down 3–0. You've just got to keep the faith. The game is not over until the last out.

—**David Ortiz**, *athlete*

Don't let others put thoughts into your mind that take away your self-confidence.

—Katori Hall, *playwright*

Either try not, or persevere.

—Ovid, *poet*

One day I realized that it didn't matter whether people loved me or not. I was released of all that insecurity when I released myself from that hope or that fantasy or whatever that yearning is and came to the conclusion that I could be happy making music regardless of whether I was successful or not. It was just a release of concern about whether I was popular or not or whether people liked me or not. It was just irrelevant to me all of a sudden.

—Shirley Manson, *musician/actor*

Do your thing and don't care if they like it.

—Tina Fey, *actor*

You have no control over other people's taste, so focus on staying true to your own.

—**Tim Gunn**, *writer/television personality*

It's YOUR VOICE. Cherish it. Respect it. Nurture it. Challenge it. Stretch it and scream until it's fucking gone. Because everyone is blessed with at least that, and who knows how long it will last.

—**Dave Grohl**, *musician*

We have all a better guide in ourselves, if we would attend to it, than any other person can be.

—Jane Austen, *writer*

I don't have ugly ducklings turning into swans in my stories. I have ugly ducklings turning into confident ducks.

—Maeve Binchy, *writer*

Don't be intimidated by what you don't know. That can be your greatest strength and ensure that you do things differently from everyone else.

—Sara Blakely, *entrepreneur*

No name-calling truly bites deep unless, in some dark part of us, we believe it. If we are confident enough then it is just noise.

—**Laurell K. Hamilton,** *writer*

Confidence is the sexiest thing a woman can have. It's much sexier than any body part.

—**Aimee Mullins**, *athlete/actor*

An important tool against self-doubt is just to ignore it. Forge ahead anyway. Just keep going, keep going, keep going.

—**Lauren Graham**, *actor*

If you don't like the road you're walking, start paving another one.

—Dolly Parton, *musician*

In playing ball, and in life, a person occasionally gets the opportunity to do something great. When that time comes, only two things matter: being prepared to seize the moment and having the courage to take your best swing.

—Hank Aaron, *athlete*

Do not be afraid of being wrong; just be afraid of being uninteresting.

—**Carl Whitmer**, *composer*

The point is not to take the world's opinion as a guiding star but to go one's way in life and work unerringly, neither depressed by failure nor seduced by applause.

—**Gustav Mahler**, *composer*

I personally know that I'm capable of whatever I put my mind to, whether someone agrees with that or not is not a concern of mine.

—**Lupita Nyong'o**, *actor*

To be yourself in a world that is constantly trying to make you something else is the greatest accomplishment.

—**Ralph Waldo Emerson**, *writer*

You are the only person on earth who can use your ability.

—**Zig Ziglar**, *writer/salesperson*

When I get hostile reactions, it really rubs me up, I love it. It's that feeling of being onstage and you're getting spit at, and you spit back!

—**Danny Elfman**, *composer*

We think confidence causes success, but it's more often a result of success— mastering something hard or accomplishing something meaningful.

—Adam Grant, *author/professor*

There is a fine line between arrogance and self-confidence. Legitimate self-confidence is a winner. The true test of self-confidence is the courage to be open—to welcome change and new ideas regardless of their source. Self-confident people aren't afraid to have their views challenged. They relish the intellectual combat that enriches ideas.

—Jack Welch, *business executive*

I've learned to ignore the negative people and just be a living example of confidence and self-love.

—**Khoudia Diop**, *model*

You can't connect the dots looking forward; you can only connect them looking backward. So you have to trust that the dots will somehow connect in your future. You have to trust in something—your gut, destiny, life, karma, whatever. Because believing that the dots will connect down the road will give you the confidence to follow your heart even when it leads you off the well-worn path; and that will make all the difference.

—**Steve Jobs,** *entrepreneur*

To free us from
the expectations of
others, to give us
back to ourselves—
there lies the great,
the singular power
of self-respect.

—Joan Didion, *writer*

Am I good enough? Yes, I am.

—Michelle Obama, *attorney/writer*

If I'm not on my
side . . .
why should
anyone else be?

—**Robert Downey Jr.,** *actor*

You still have
a lot of time to
make yourself be
what you want.

—S. E. Hinton, *writer*

You can see
yourself as
a wave in
the ocean or
you can see
yourself as
the ocean.

—**Oprah Winfrey,** *media executive*

You grow through failures in life, not the wins. And, as you grow, you become more self-assured around your own abilities and qualities, and that's how you start collecting confidence.

—**Kim Gravel**, *business executive/writer*

Don't let anyone tell you what you can or cannot do, or cannot achieve. Do not allow it.

—**Emma Watson**, *actor*

If you know you are on the right track, if you have this inner knowledge, then nobody can turn you off . . . no matter what they say.

—**Barbara McClintock**, *scientist*

Sometimes you climb out of bed in the morning and you think, I'm not going to make it, but you laugh inside remembering all the times you've felt that way.

—**Charles Bukowski**, *writer*

Nothing is impossible;
there are ways that
lead to everything. . . .
It is often merely for
an excuse that we say
things are impossible.

—François de La Rochefoucauld,
essayist

The only way to build self-confidence is to take a risk and take action despite your fear of failure, messing up or embarrassment. If things work out, then you now know you can do more than you think. If things don't work out, you now know that you can *handle* more than you think. Either way, you're better off.

—**Alex Malley**, *business executive*

Belief in oneself and knowing who you are, I mean, that's the foundation for everything great.

—Jay-Z, *rapper/producer*

The most beautiful thing you can wear is confidence.

—**Blake Lively**, *actor*

What you are looking for is already in you. . . . You already are everything you are seeking.

—Thích Nhất Hạnh, *monk/peace activist*

Your self-worth is determined by you. You don't have to depend on someone to tell you who you are.

—**Beyoncé**, *singer/songwriter*

You have to have insane confidence in yourself, even if it's not real. You need to be your own cheerleader now, because there isn't a room full of people waiting with pom-poms to tell you, "You did it! We've been waiting all this time for you to succeed!"

—**Mindy Kaling,** *actor*

I can control my thoughts, so why am I disturbed? Whatever is outside my thoughts has no effect. Learn this, and you can live well; you can remake yourself.

—**Marcus Aurelius,** *emperor*

Don't ever
stop believing
in yourself.
You're amazing,
and don't let
anyone tell you
otherwise.

—**Chiara Mingarelli**, *astrophysicist*

You either
walk inside
your story and
own it or you
stand outside
your story and
hustle for your
worthiness.

—Brené Brown, *professor/writer*

There is one path in the world that none can walk but you. Where does it lead? Don't ask, walk!

—**Friedrich Nietzsche**, *philosopher*

The worst thing in the world is to want to be popular. I can't give you a recipe for success, but I can give you a recipe for failure: try to please everybody. You should live your life as you wish. Particularly in these years I have a much more "live and let live" attitude about life than I had when I was younger. I let people be who they want to be and I will be who I am. I am less judgmental.

—Frank Langella, *actor*

Deserve your dream.

—Octavio Paz, *poet/diplomat*

I think if anyone tells you the odds are slim, just keep walking. Just do whatever the hell you want to do, because they don't know what they're talking about. When you love something, and you work really really hard at it, you can do it.

—**Melissa McCarthy**, *comedian*

It doesn't matter what other people think. Not everyone is going to always support you 100% but as long as you are doing you and you know that you're becoming a better person then that's what's important.

—**Gwen Jorgensen**, *athlete*

You can vanquish the demons only when you yourself are convinced of your own worth.

—**Adeline Yen Mah**, *writer*

People are capable, at any time in their lives, of doing what they dream of.

—**Paulo Coelho,** *writer*

Learn to embrace your own unique beauty, celebrate your unique gifts with confidence. Your imperfections are actually a gift.

—Kerry Washington, *actor*

You got a chance to go up and say something? Don't be shy. No matter how it comes out, just let it come out.

—**Fiona Apple**, *singer/songwriter*

I discovered that rejections are not altogether a bad thing. They teach a writer to rely on his own judgment and to say in his heart of hearts, "To hell with you."

—**Saul Bellow**, *writer*

Only those who will risk going too far can possibly find out just how far one can go.

—T. S. Eliot, *poet*

Brave doesn't mean you're not scared. . . . It means you go on even though you're scared.

—**Angie Thomas,** *writer*

If we listened to our intellect, we'd never have a love affair. We'd never have a friendship. We'd never go in business because we'd be cynical. . . . Well, that's nonsense. You're going to miss life. You've got to jump off the cliff all the time and build your wings on the way down.

—**Ray Bradbury**, *writer*

Maybe you have a little voice inside that says you aren't strong enough to handle what life has left at your feet. That voice lies. Prove it wrong today—then repeat, repeat, repeat. Keep moving. That voice lies. Prove it wrong today—then repeat, repeat, repeat. Keep moving.

—Maggie Smith, *poet/writer/editor*

Be yourself. The world worships the original.

—John Gay, *writer*

Believe in yourself. You've got to take that chance, even if it's hard, even if it doesn't make sense: Just believe in yourself. Even if you don't, pretend that you do and, at some point, you will. With self-belief comes self-esteem, as well. All of those things contribute to making good decisions for yourself. That's so important for young women.

—Venus Williams, *athlete*

Your magic is there, if only you would let it be instead of fighting it all the time.

—**Christina Henry**, *writer*

I have gone through a long apprenticeship. I have gone through enough of being a nobody. I have decided that when I am a star, I will be every inch and every moment the star!

—**Gloria Swanson**, *actor*

You change
the world
by being
yourself.

—Yoko Ono, *artist*

There's always going to be somebody smarter, prettier, nicer. It's better to appreciate it instead of being threatened by it or defending yourself against it.

—**Mary Louise Parker**, *actor*

I've always done whatever I want and always been exactly who I am.

—**Billie Eilish**, *singer/songwriter*

Always be yourself, express yourself, have faith in yourself. Do not go out and look for a successful personality and duplicate him.

—**Bruce Lee**, *athlete*

I prefer to be true to myself, even at the hazard of incurring the ridicule of others, rather than to be false, and incur my own abhorrence.

—**Frederick Douglass,**
activist/writer/statesman

I never loved another person the way I loved myself.

—**Mae West**, *actor*

You have to have confidence in your vision or else no one else will trust in it.

—**Mary Katrantzou**, *designer*

Accept right now that you are magnificent.

—Gabby Bernstein,
writer/motivational speaker

So shut up,
live, travel,
adventure,
bless and don't
be sorry.

—Jack Kerouac, *writer*

I always say you should be very careful with the voices you listen to. And my closest voices have always told me, "You can."

—**Becky Hammon**, *coach*

The people who
are crazy enough
to think they can
change the world
are the ones who do.

—**Steve Jobs**, *entrepreneur*

You can do hard things.
You will get through,
you will make a decision
and one day you will
look back and think,
"Remember when?"

—**Rachel Marie Martin**, *writer*

Don't fear difficult moments. The best comes from them.

—Rita Levi-Montalcini, *neurobiologist*

Yes, it's a jungle out here, but it's a jungle everywhere. Life, in fact, is just one big wilderness. But you were born for this wilderness, and you have the instruments to negotiate it safely.

—**Martha Beck**, *writer*

If I'd had children and had a girl, the first words I would have taught her would have been "fuck off" because we weren't brought up ever to say that to anyone, were we? And it's quite valuable to have the courage and the confidence to say, "No, fuck off, leave me alone, thank you very much." You see, I couldn't help saying "Thank you very much," I just couldn't help myself.

—Helen Mirren, *actor*

Anything scares me, anything scares anyone but really after all considering how dangerous everything is nothing is really very frightening.

—**Gertrude Stein**, *writer*

The best thing about your life is that it is constantly in a state of design. This means you have, at all times, the power to redesign it. Make moves, allow shifts, smile more, do more, do less, say no, say yes—just remember, when it comes to your life, you are not only the artist but the masterpiece as well.

—Cleo Wade, *writer*

Here is the world.
Beautiful and terrible
things will happen.
Don't be afraid.

—**Frederick Buechner**, *writer/theologian*

Be scared. You can't help that. But don't be afraid. Ain't nothing in the woods going to hurt you unless you corner it, or it smells that you are afraid. A bear or a deer, too, has got to be scared of a coward the same as a brave man has got to be.

—William Faulkner, *writer*

Confidence. If you have it, you can make anything look good.

—Diane von Furstenberg, *designer*

Our greatest problems in life come not so much from the situations we confront as from our doubts about our ability to handle them.

—**Susan L. Taylor,** *editor/journalist*

Don't be afraid to be afraid.

—Madeleine L'Engle, *writer*

To be hopeful, to embrace one possibility after another—that is surely the basic instinct. . . . Crying out: High tide! . . . Time to move out into the glorious debris. Time to take this life for what it is!

—**Barbara Kingsolver,** *writer*

Self-belief does not necessarily ensure success, but self-disbelief assuredly spawns failure.

—**Albert Bandura**, *psychologist*

What people hate most is indecision. Even if I'm completely unsure, I'll pretend I know exactly what I'm talking about and make a decision.

—**Anna Wintour,** *editor*

I say, follow your bliss and don't be afraid, and doors will open where you didn't know they were going to be.

—**Joseph Campbell,** *writer*

Don't let anyone tell you that you can't do something, but especially not yourself. Go conquer the world. Just remember this: Why not you?

—**Mindy Kaling,** *actor*

I had a massive ego. Massive. But that's not such a bad thing. Because at least you're aspiring to be something, you consider yourself great because you want to be great.

—**Prince**, *musician*

Our doubts are traitors, And make us lose the good we oft might win, by fearing to attempt.

—William Shakespeare, *writer*

Stop making excuses, you're the only one stopping you.

—**Issa Rae**, *actor/writer/producer*

Pretend that this is a time of miracles and we believe in them.

—**Edwidge Danticat**, *writer*

Confidence is ultimately about being comfortable in a wide variety of situations that would make most people feel uncomfortable. So if you stretch your comfort zone every day, very quickly you'll have a large comfort zone and be able to feel more comfortable even when outside of it.

—**Charlie Houpert**, *lifestyle coach*

As soon as you trust yourself, you will know how to live.

—Johann Wolfgang von Goethe,
writer/scientist

Everything you've ever wanted is sitting on the other side of fear.

—George Addair,
motivational writer/real estate developer

I am learning every day to allow the space between where I am and where I want to be to inspire me and not terrify me.

—Tracee Ellis Ross, *actor/producer*

One truth I have discovered for sure: When you believe that all things are possible and you are willing to work hard to accomplish your goals, you can achieve the next "impossible" dream. No dream is too high!

—**Buzz Aldrin**, *astronaut*

When you doubt your power, you give power to your doubt.

—Honoré de Balzac, *writer*

For the only safe harbor in this life's tossing, troubled sea is to refuse to be bothered about what the future will bring and to stand ready and confident, squaring the breast to take without skulking or flinching whatever fortune hurls at us.

—**Seneca**, *philosopher*

Confidence is a state of mind, necessary to succeed, and the starting point of developing self-confidence is definiteness of purpose.

—Andrew Carnegie,
business executive/philanthropist

All success in life starts within you. You know what to do. You know how to do it. Your next step is simple. You are the first domino.

—**Gary W. Keller**, *entrepreneur/writer*

Even though so much seems to be in pieces, trust your wholeness. Accept that you cannot be sure of everything, but be sure of yourself.

—**Maggie Smith**, *poet/writer/editor*

Do you really want to look back on your life and see how wonderful it could have been had you not been afraid to live it?

—Caroline Myss, *writer*

Randall Linke

About the Authors

Kathryn & Ross Petras, sister and brother writing team, are *New York Times* bestselling authors, NPR syndicated radio hosts, and quotation connoisseurs. Among their most popular collections of quotations are the books *"It Always Seems Impossible Until It's Done."* and *"Dance First, Think Later."*